OPERATION MINCEMEAT

The Untold World War II Story of How One Corpse Led to the Nazis' Defeat

By R.C. Bread

Note from the Author:

Thank you for supporting my book, *Operation Mincemeat: The Untold World War 2 Story of How One Corpse Led to the Nazis' Defeat* !

I hope you will enjoy learning about this unique World War 2 story! This is my first book I published, and I am so excited and thankful for this opportunity.

After reading this, I would love your support and hope that you could take a moment to post an honest review on Amazon. I am eager to hear from you because it will help me improve this book and others in the future.

Thank you so much for your time and support! It really means a lot!

TABLE OF CONTENTS

Ewen Montagu
Charles Cholmondeley
Jean Leslie (AKA "Pam")
Ian Fleming
Glyndwr Michael

References

OPTION 2: AUDIO BOOK

If you prefer to listen to audiobooks, you can instead listen to the free audiobook version through two ways:

1. Emailing rcbreadhistory@gmail.com and typing either in the subject or the body of the message "Operation Mincemeat." Within 48 hours you will receive a folder containing the entire book in audiobook format (with multiple speeds inside too).

2. Using the table of contents and list found below which contains the links of the audio book files. For this, you will need to request access, which I will promptly give within 48 hours of the request. If you request for one audiobook file, you will be granted access to all of the audiobook files automatically.

You will have the option to listen to the audio book and can choose what speed you would prefer.

The options and links to the speeds are below:

- **1x Speed:**   https://rb.gy/gai3g

- **1.5x Speed:**   https://rb.gy/a1tcg

- **1.75x Speed:**   https://rb.gy/ecpvv

- **2x Speed:**   https://rb.gy/zqf7m

- **3x Speed:**   https://rb.gy/ud2ka

- **All Speeds Folder:** https://rb.gy/0yv2q

Note: You will also get exclusive access to information and other bonuses for future books!

INTRODUCTION AND BACKGROUND

At the beginning of World War II, Hitler quickly captured massive amounts of land. Through his blitzkrieg tactic, where he quickly invaded nations with large, concentrated amounts of airplanes and tanks, he could conquer and cover 120 miles of land in just five days. First, he took Czechoslovakia, then Poland, and the list goes on. For the major nations he did not overtake, he allied with them. With this style of conquest, just one year after the Blitzkrieg of Czechoslovakia, he either controlled or was allied with the vast majority of Europe. His conquest continued, and the Allied powers stood up to fight against him.

For a year, the Axis forces dominated, constantly seizing land after land. Eventually though, Hitler started to taste defeat and loss. His first major setback was against the USSR, a nation he formerly signed an armistice with before eventually breaking his promise and invading them. Hitler initially experienced lots of success, capturing over 2 million Russian soldiers and burrowing through the Russian landscape. However, due to an early winter and strong USSR resistance, the Axis forces were unprepared, and Stalin could fight back, thus forcing the Axis powers to retreat.

Even further, in the summer of 1942, the British defeated General Erwin Rommel's troops at El Alamein, leading to a major retreat for the Axis forces located there. By May 1943, the German and Italian forces located there had surrendered. Hitler's invincible aura seemed to be fading.

In order to further break down the Axis's forces, the Allies wanted to open another front on the European side of the war. At the moment, there was only one front on the USSR side. The most obvious target was Italy. Italy was weakly defended in relation to other areas, and the recently finished North African campaign left many troops at the top of Africa, ready to attack Italy. In fact, Churchill, the Prime Minister of Britain, even referred to Italy as the "soft underbelly of Europe" as a reference to its slightly weaker defenses. In the best-case scenario, an invasion of Italy could remove a major Axis power from the war, Mussolini, and provide a path that could eventually lead to Germany. In the worst-case scenario, it would divert and divide Hitler's forces. By diverting these forces, it would ease up the pressure on the USSR's front of the war and could even decrease the defenses in France, the target for the D-Day invasion.

In order to get to Italy, it would be best to first take Sicily, a nearby island. Sicily would be perfect for allowing the Allies to regroup and prepare their forces before making the final assault on Italy. The only issue was that this plan was too obvious. Both the Allies and the Axis powers knew how crucial Sicily was, and the Axis powers would defend it as such. The only way to make a decent assault on Sicily, and therefore Italy, would be to use deceit to trick the Axis nations into thinking the assault was somewhere else: the Balkans.

The Balkans were another likely target for the Allies as it would allow them to invade Greece and apply pressure on the Germans near the Eastern Front. Even better, the Balkans had minerals that the Germans needed, so an attack there would not be completely unpredictable. The Allies wanted to create a trick that convinced the Germans and Italians of a fake attack in the Balkans in order to divert the majority of their defenses away from Sicily.

In one of the most successful military deceptions of the 20th century, the Allies came up with a plan to create a fake corpse disguised as a British Royal Marines officer, and plant it with falsified information of an attack not on Sicily, but on the Balkans.

The Allies ensured this corpse ended up in German spies' hands, creating a chain reaction that diverted the defenses of Sicily. This is the story of how the death of one homeless Welsh impacted the course of an entire World War.

R.C. BREAD

CHAPTER 1:
EVENTS LEADING
UP TO OPERATION
MINCEMEAT

The origin of this plan was first found in the Trout Memo. The Trout Memo was written by Rear Admiral John Godfrey, but it has been suspected that most of the ideas actually originated from his assistant, Lieutenant Commander Ian Fleming. The Memo was initially written on September 29th, 1939, and circulated throughout British intelligence.

The Trout Memo was a compilation of military strategies and plans that could be used to deceive and trick an enemy. The Memo compares the aspects of deceiving an enemy to the effort of fly-fishing. A part of the Trout Memo reads, "The Trout Fisher casts patiently all day. He frequently changes his venue and his lures. If he has frightened a fish he may 'give the water a rest for half-an-hour,' but his main endeavor, viz. to attract fish by something he sends out from his boat, is incessant."

The Trout Memo contained 54 unique ways to deceive an enemy, but only number 28, the original inspiration for Operation Mincemeat, is thought to have been used. The idea was quite broad and was actually noted to be "not a very nice one."

The Trout Memo says this in regard to the idea:
"The following suggestion is used in a book by Basil Thomson: a

corpse dressed as an airman, with despatches in his pockets, could be dropped on the coast, supposedly from a parachute that has failed. I understand there is no difficulty in obtaining corpses at the Naval Hospital, but, of course, it would have to be a fresh one."

Previous Successes

In no way was the Trout Memo the originator of the idea to put falsified documents in the enemies' hands. In fact, the British had used this type of tactic before in previous wars and were quite familiar with it. One of the first instances of them using this tactic was during the First World War, when the British put falsified documents inside haversack bags and left them for the enemy to discover. This plan had fooled the Ottomans on multiple occasions and was particularly effective in the Battle of Beersheba.

The first time the British used a corpse to mislead was during the Battle of Alam el Halfa in the summer of 1942. On top of the corpse, the British planted false maps that demonstrated the location of supposed minefields. Through this, the maps led the Germans into a specific area where they could be easily attacked.

Furthermore, recently acquired information made it even easier to enact the plan. In September 1942, the British learned that sensitive documents and information that ended up in Spain, a neutral nation, were being given to German spies to copy down and analyze before eventually being sent back to the Allies. This information was essential to the mission, as it was the ultimate location of where the corpse was placed.

The British found out about this information leak because of a British plane crash that was headed to Gibraltar, near Cadiz. The fallen plane had a courier who had sensitive information and a French spy to accompany him. After the Spanish recovered the body, they sent it quickly back to Britain with all the materials found near the body. Although the contents of the courier appeared not to be opened, it was confirmed later by British intelligence that the notebook that the French spy had was copied completely by the Germans. This confirmed to the Allies that information found in Spain was distributed to the Germans under the radar before sending it back to the Allies. With this, the idea started to form and appear.

Approving the Plan

The plan for Operation Mincemeat was originally proposed by Charles Cholmondeley, an officer of the Royal Air Force and also working for the MI5 counterintelligence agency as an additional post. Around one month after the British confirmed the information leaks in Spain, Charles started to brainstorm for a new tactic similar to the one mentioned in the Trout Memo.

The new plan was originally referred to as the "Trojan Horse," and Charles took the idea from the Trout Memo and added other details to make it more realistic. In his idea proposition to the MI5, Charles writes:

"A body is obtained from one of the London hospitals ... The lungs are filled with water and documents are disposed in an inside pocket. The body is then dropped by a Coastal Command aircraft ... On being found, the supposition in the enemy's mind may well be that one of our aircraft has either been shot or forced down and that this is one of their passengers."

Charles was the secretary of the Twenty Committee, an exclusive team of intelligence officers whose job was to manage double agents that operated inside enemy ranks. When he finished the plan, he submitted it to the committee, but he was met with disagreement. The committee thought the plan was simply unrealistic and impossible to implement in a real-world scenario, as there were too many uncertainties and unpredictable factors in dropping the corpse from a plane.

Image of Charles Cholmondeley during war times; image from World War II Database
https://ww2db.com/image.php?image_id=26229

However, they did not completely reject it, and instead, a new idea emerged. The alternative plan was instead to make the operation a naval one instead of one based in the air. The original idea, where they simply chucked the corpse out of the aircraft, was replaced with one where the body would be dumped in the ocean, making it easier to control the variables and conditions of the corpse.

The new plan got the green light, and Cholmondeley was assigned a partner from the Royal Navy to assist with the project. The chosen partner for Cholmondeley was Ewen Montagu, a member of the Naval Intelligence Division and a direct subordinate of Admiral Godfrey. Montagu was a lawyer before joining the war effort, but in the war, apart from running the division's counterintelligence, he also oversaw all double agents working for the navy on deception operations. Having the plan approved and the leaders for the operation determined, Operation Mincemeat had just begun.

Image of Ewen Montagu during war times; Image from World War II Database https://ww2db.com/image.php?image_id=26226

R.C. BREAD

CHAPTER 2: MAKING WILLIAM MARTIN

As mentioned earlier, there were really two main areas that Hitler suspected the Allies would attack: The Balkans or Sicily. While Sicily allowed the opportunity to attack and invade Italy, the Balkans allowed the opportunity to attack Greece and eventually help the Eastern Front. Even further, the Germans needed minerals in the Balkans, so Hitler ensured that this area was well defended. The Allies intended to use this paranoia and fear to their advantage.

In order to reinforce Hitler's focus on the Balkans, the Allies used Operation Barclay. Operation Barclay was a series of fake military maneuvers to trick the Axis powers into thinking the next attack was in Greece. They had staged radio communications, had military maps of Greece and made it as public as they could, and even hired Greek translators meant to be interpreted as preparation for an attack on Greece. All of these actions were used to make Hitler think that there was going to be an imminent attack on the Balkans and Greece.

The Allies even created a fake formation called the 12th Army, which consisted of twelve non-existent divisions in the Eastern Mediterranean. The British established a supposed headquarters for this division in Egypt, which was near the Balkans. To further support the ruse, the Allies also had maneuver and military drills in Syria. In these drills, the Allies used a mixture of real forces and fake-dummy vehicles that looked real from a distance. Meanwhile, the real mission for Operation Husky, where the Allies actually attacked Sicily, was being prepared for in Tunisia, where the communication was minimized through the use of landlines to keep secrecy.

All these ruses proved to be successful, and the Germans started to divert their forces to the Balkans already. However, while some forces were moved, the final push from Operation Mincemeat would be the final straw to convince Hitler to dedicate all of his forces to that area.

Now, despite it being during war, finding a body for Operation Mincemeat was quite difficult. There were many requirements that they had to meet. Creating a new, fake identity was hard enough, but finding a corpse that was physically suitable was also incredibly difficult. Even further, nobody would offer the body of a deceased loved one to be thrown into the sea for the operation, despite how important it could be. This meant that Montagu and Cholmondeley had to find a body belonging to someone with no relatives, family, or friends.

Finding and Acquiring a Suitable Body

Despite the surplus of bodies from the war, none of them could reasonably be used. It was simply disrespectful and rude to use the body of a veteran who served and died for the country. Montagu and Cholmondeley also had to find the body of someone who not only wasn't a veteran but was recently deceased and whose body could be preserved for a decent amount of time as preparations were being made. They also had to worry about the manner of death for the body in order to make the body more convincing. They prepared to have a corpse that might have some scratches or perhaps symptoms of drowning. Montagu and Cholmondeley asked and went to numerous morgues, hospitals, and other locations in order to find a body that would meet all these requirements.

In their search and planning, Montagu and Cholmondeley came across Bernard Spilsbury, a pathologist, through the guidance of

Major Frank Foley of the British MI6 Secret Intelligence Service. They asked Spilsbury for insights into choosing a dead body for Operation Mincemeat. They knew that the Nazis would most likely analyze the body before anything else, so they needed the body to be absolutely perfect, and Spilsbury provided invaluable information to them. Spilsbury advised against filling the body's lungs with water, as was initially planned. He instead said that in a plane crash, the cause of death would more likely be shock rather than drowning.

Image of Bernard Spilsbury during the 1920s; image from wikemedia commons https://commons.wikimedia.org/wiki/File:BernardSpilsbury.jpg

The intelligence officers, after conversing with Spilsbury, went to Sir Bentley Purchase, a coroner of the North District of London. As the coroner, he had jurisdiction over nearly all of London and was the perfect person to ask for a suitable corpse. However, Purchase made it clear to them that obtaining such a corpse would be no easy task, mainly due to the legal and practical reasons of the assignment. Nevertheless, he promised to lookout for such a body and report to Montagu and his team as soon as a possible candidate popped up.

The news for such a body came in late January, 1943, when Purchase told Montagu of a body fulfilling the requirements. The body was from a Welsh vagrant by the name of Glyndwr Michael. Michael is thought to have died of suicide through the consumption of rat poison and wasn't able to get saved in time. While rat poison is usually traceable during an inspection, an extensive examination of the body determined that the poison levels were low, and they would get lower and lower over time, especially when the body would float in the ocean. Even better, Spilsbury mentioned that the Spaniard pathologist in Huelva wouldn't be as well trained or experienced as Spilsbury, and so with such a low concentration of rat poison, it would be nearly impossible for a pathologist of that level to figure out and detect the plot.

Cholmondeley and Montagu agreed to use the body and accepted Purchase's offer. The only issue with it was that the corpse was rather unfit and skinny, especially for the body of a troop, making it suspicious. Regardless, they agreed on using the body and started with the plan. The body could not be frozen, but needed to be kept relatively fresh for the mission to work. Therefore, the Allies put the body in a fridge and got right to work. They would have to create a completely new identity for this man, or they would have to find a completely new corpse.

The Birth of Major William Martin

By February of 1943, Montagu and Cholmondeley finalized the final plan for the Operation and submitted the plan to the Twenty Committee, which was quickly approved and given the green light.

As the Allies could have made the body land in Italian Territory, where it would have surely ended up in German hands, it was a more obvious ploy that could have been found out. Spain was chosen because it was deemed to be a neutral country, and thus it would be less suspicious if a body drifted ashore. Despite its neutrality, with the recent confirmation that British bodies that ended up in Spanish territory were searched and documented by the Germans, Spain became the prime location. It was both inconspicuous and guaranteed.

The next order of business with Montagu was creating the body's fake identity that was detailed, convincing, and verifiable. The imaginary person's rank was decided to be a Royal Marine Officer, which would allow some level of clearance to privy information on planned operations in Europe. They determined this man to also be named William Martin and was given a post at the Combined Operations Headquarters as a Captain who was acting as Major. The name was similar enough to a number of other officers in the Royal Marines, which made the fake identity hard to disprove.

Another advantage of Martin being a Royal Marine was that the Royal Marines were under the management of the Admiralty of the British Government, which allowed for the agents of Operation Mincemeat to keep track of any questions and investigations regarding William Martin's identity. If someone sought to confirm his death and identity, the inquiries would be right in the Naval Intelligence Division's hands, which made it much easier to control the flow of information and deceit.

R.C. BREAD

CHAPTER 3: FINAL PREPARATIONS AND PLAN EXECUTION

Although Martin's broad identity was secured, Montagu and Cholmondeley had to go much further in order to convince the Axis powers that Martin was truly a real person. They had to add the smallest, seemingly irrelevant details to make him appear natural and believable. Spies often engaged in this type of routine practice, often called "pocket" or "wallet litter." For instance, the British spies created an entirely new, fake person, who was deemed to be Martin's fiancée. They decided to call this woman Pam and even had a photo of this supposed person. The person that they took to fake this identity was a lady who worked with the officers of MI5, named Jean Leslie. The Mincemeat operatives asked women in the MI5 to send them photos, and the one selected was Jean Leslie's photo. The photo was deemed to be a more "personal" photo that Martin kept as comfort.

The Photo of Pam(Jean Leslie) Used in the Operation; image from Wikemedia commons   https:// commons.wikimedia.org/wiki/File:UK_National_Archives_-_WO_1065921.jpg

The duties of Jean Leslie were more than simply a photo, though. In order to concretely prove William Martin and Pam's relationship, they had to create a true relationship and events in it. It was found that Jean Leslie and Ewen Montagu roleplayed Pam and William, respectively, and watched at the cinema and even danced together. They wrote fake love letters to each other, signing the letters by "Bill" and "Pam." It was also planned that Wiliam Martin would propose to Pam soon after the war, and they included a receipt of a diamond ring from a real jewelry shop in London to ensure the Germans could track it down if needed. Because of all the events and activities Ewen and Pam engaged in, some historians suspect that the roleplaying of the characters went beyond just simple acting and that there might have been a hint of true romance there.

In addition to Martin's relationship with Pam, the spies of Operation Mincemeat also faked a letter from his father and other relations to increase the depth of Martin's character. Of course, they used certain inks to avoid them being washed off from the time the body would spend in the water.

Martin's pocket litter included a variety of other items that would be common in an Officer of the Marines. They planted little items such as cigarettes, matches, pencils, keys, a silver cross, and a small receipt. They even had items that linked to real places, such as theater tickets and hotel bills, to add to Martin's validity as a person. They made sure that if the Germans and Italians really wanted to, they could track down Martin to his daily life.

Some of Martin's pocket litter found on him; image from World War II Database https://ww2db.com/image.php?image_id=26253

The last essential pocket litter that was necessary to Martin was his fake navy ID. Initially, Montagu and Cholmondeley tried to take a photo of Glyndwr directly, but it was nearly impossible to make him look alive. They instead were faced with a dilemma because they needed someone that looked like the dead man before them. This duty fell upon Ronnie Reed, a captain in the MI5.

The last step for this ID was to make it look worn out, since a brand-new card could easily arouse suspicion. In order to counteract this, Montagu kept the ID documents with him over the weeks before the mission commenced and periodically rubbed them on his trousers to give the appearance of being used and natural. This was so necessary because during that time, many personal documents were made of paper, and therefore would be impossible to look brand new in practice, especially with a supposed seasoned Royal Marine Officer like Major William Martin. The uniform that would be finally given to Martin was also given a similar treatment and was worn by Cholmondeley for a while.

The fake identity card for William Martin; image from wikemedia commons https://commons.wikimedia.org/wiki/File:Major_Martin.jpg

Falsifying the Invasion

The difficult part of the mission was not only creating William Martin but also authentically hinting about an attack in the Balkans. Cholmondeley had to fabricate letters and plans out of nowhere in order to make the plans convincing.

There were several documents in the package, such as one from Lieutenant General Sir Archibald Nye, the vice chief of the British Imperial General Staff. The letter was written as if it were sent from General Sir Harold Alexander, commander of the 18th Army Group stationed in North Africa, who was also a direct subordinate to General Eisenhower.

In the beginning, Montagu and the spies tried to fabricate a letter on their own, but it was deemed to be unconvincing and unnatural for the high echelons of Allied command. Montagu decided that three requirements must be met for this letter. First, it would have to state that the Balkans were the target of a main assault, but also say it in a casual and natural way. Second, the letter would have to speak of Sicily as if it were a cover for the main invasion of Greece. Lastly, the letter had to be personal and unofficial.

After several attempts, the team gave up trying to fabricate it, and asked Archibald himself to write the letter. The letter he wrote was perfect for the mission, being both efficient and optimal. It touched upon a few different topics, some of which were deemed to be classified or sensitive at least, but regardless, Montagu and his spies were quite satisfied with the result. The most crucial section of Nye's writing was when he mentioned intelligence reports of German reinforcements in Greece and Crete and stated that these reinforcements were a "concern" because the Imperial General Staff thought that the Allied forces in North Africa were insufficient. The letter even further discussed and recommended reinforcements for these troops, implying an Ally attack on Greece since they were so carefully considering the Axis build-up in the Balkans.

Another crucial document that strengthened Martin's identity was one written by Vice-Admiral Louis Mountbatten, his supposed superior. It was crucial in further solidifying his identity and gave some reference and details about Martin, such as being a specialist in amphibious warfare and crucial in the next invasion. This masterful letter both strengthened Martin's identity and supported the invasion of the Balkans.

Letter from Louis Mountbatten to William Martin; image from World War II Database
https://ww2db.com/image.php?image_id=26225

In order to be able to tell if the Spanish had actually opened the letter, they used an effectively simple system. The system was simply placing an eyelash into the envelope. If the envelope was opened, the eyelash would be gone, and the Allies would know it had been tampered with. If the eyelash was still there, they knew the Axis powers did not end up going through the information.

Lastly, in order to tie up the final arrangements for William Martin, Montagu's spies planted all the most important documents into a briefcase, just in case the Catholic Spaniards decided not to search the corpse itself. Securing a briefcase allowed all the documents to remain firmly with Martin, and it was also not unnatural at the time because it was common for briefcases with important items to be chained to their holders.

Last Steps and Implementation

The location where the body was to be deployed was Huelva, which is on Spain's southern coast, near the Portuguese border. Portugal and France were evaluated as potential options, but Montagu decided in the end that Huelva was the most suitable choice due to the local currents and tides. Additionally, the Allies had confirmed at least one German spy in the area. The spy's name was Adolf Clauss, an agent of the Abwehr and the son of the German consul in Spain. He was also known to have important connections with the local authorities, which would ensure that he would be able to find and have access to the corpse. The British also had connections in the area with their own consulate, so there was a way to have additional logistic support on site.

The initial plan was for Martin to die from a plane crash, but it was ultimately decided by Montagu to use a submarine to deliver the corpse. They initially wanted to simulate the plane crash with flares and other means, but this approach was found to have obvious problems and the potential to compromise the ruse. The team also thought of using surface vessels, but it was thought to be too open and revealing. A submarine was deemed to be the perfect fit for the mission, as it could quickly and quietly deliver the body into Spanish waters and then disappear.

With all the details finalized, Montagu's team promptly presented the draft to the Chief of Staff Committee on April 13, 1943. It went all the way up to Winston Churchill through Colonel John Bevan, the overseer of all deception work. Colonel John Bevan informed Churchill of all the risks, and after consideration, Churchill gave the approval as long as General Eisenhower agreed with the plan. Just four days after it was submitted, on April 17th, Eisenhower gave the greenlight for the operation to proceed.

Operation Mincemeat commenced immediately after it was approved, in the early hours of April 17th. However, despite all the preparation and dedication they spent on the project, they already ran into an issue. As they were taking Major William Martin's body out of the specialized preservation container, they found that the feet froze. Due to the stiffness of it, putting the necessary boots on became nearly impossible, and they had to defrost this part of the body in order to put it on. Once they put on the boot, they immediately put it in the last special container to store it, which was filled with dry ice and contained no oxygen.

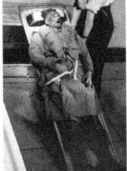

The body used in Operation Mincemeat right before being put in the canister; image from World War II Database https://ww2db.com/image.php?image_id=26227

The container with the body in it was first transported by van to Greenock, Scotland. The driver of the van was none other than John "Jock" Horsfall, a former racecar driver that was hired by the Security Service to drive and transport spies. He had a reputation as a more reckless driver, almost crashing numerous times while traveling at high speeds. Even more concerning was the fact that he was legally blind, yet still drove without any corrective eyewear. Either way, he was still a talented figure that performed the job perfectly.

Scotland was the location where the body boarded the submarine called HMS Seraph. Lieutenant Bill Jewell and the crew of HMS Seraph, had already participated in several deceit operations before, but was still not allowed to know what was actually in the container. Only Jewell knew the real identity of what was in the canister, and the others were simply told that it was a device for meteorological monitoring off the coast of Spain. Secrecy for this mission was of utmost importance. It all remained in the hands of Jewell as Montagu and Cholmondeley both returned to London after handing William Martin off.

The HMS Seraph departed on April 19th and sailed for ten days before they reached Huelva. The journey was no easy one, as the submarine had been spotted and bombed two times before making it to Spain. However, the mission was never compromised. On April 29th, the screw searched the area before surfacing and was finally able to surface in the early hours of April 30th. The team took out the body and placed it in the water. After reading Psalm 39, the team left and let the submarine propellers push Martin toward the Spanish coast. The one final task the team had was to dispose of the empty container used to store the body. After failing to sink it with machineguns, the men eventually used explosives to destroy it. Lieutenant Jewell then reported to the British Admiralty that the mission had been successfully finished.

Image of Charles Cholmondeley and Montagu right before their journey to Scotland; image from World War II Database https://ww2db.com/image.php?image_id=26223

R.C. BREAD

CHAPTER 4: DISCOVERY AND EFFECT

The mission was finished, and the success of it was only left to fate now. The body, as predicted, floated over to the Spanish coast, and in the early morning of April 30th, a curious fisherman stumbled upon the drifting corpse. The body was found by local fisherman Antonio Rey Maria nearby a beach called La Mata Negra

Quickly realizing that the body was one of a soldier, he decided to drag it back to land. As he later said to a friend, Antonio noticed bruising and guessed that the man may have fallen from somewhere, potentially a plane crash. The fisherman also noticed the briefcase attached to the body, which intrigued him but not enough for Antonio to meddle with it. As a good citizen, Antonio quickly reported the discovery to the authorities, and Spanish soldiers arrived to take the body away.

Initial Reactions

Once the military and authorities received the corpse, it was sent directly to the Spanish naval judge for analysis and decisions on how to proceed. The British vice-consul in Huelva, Francis Haselden, was informed by the Spanish authorities of a body of a British Officer that appeared. This was the expected formality, and Haselden quickly reported to the British authorities that confirmed the body had made its way to the Spanish.

Montagu then used deceptive communications to support

the deception. Montagu and Haselden purposely used communications via diplomatic cable, which was known to be monitored and intercepted by the Axis powers. In their communications, they intentionally used a cipher that the Germans already cracked, ensuring that the message would be translated fully. While in communication, Montagu implied that the briefcase was extremely important for strategic purposes and had to be brought back quickly and without any interception. This sense of urgency piqued the interest of Adolf Clauss, the German spy in the area.

The Spaniards had an autopsy of the body on May 1st to figure out and confirm the cause of death. This was a crucial part of the mission, where the slightest discovery could ruin the entire operation. When planning the mission, Spilsbury, the pathologist that guided Montagu and Cholmondeley, insisted that the level of the pathologist in Huelva would be relatively low and would have trouble diagnosing the cause of death as anything but drowning. However, contrary to his belief, the task fell on the experienced and knowledgeable Dr. Fernández and his son Eduardo, a recent medical school graduate. His son, Eduardo, was an intelligence researcher that would later publish a study on hypoproteinemia in liver cirrhosis, and Dr. Fernández had been examining bodies for 22 years and has seen a variety of cases, specializing in ones related to drowning due to him working nearby the coast.

Luckily, Haselden was present for the autopsy, and he used his presence to ensure the pathologists discovered as little as possible. Given the right amount of time and thoroughness, the doctors could easily discover that William Martin did not die recently and snuff out the ruse. Haselden strongly pressured the pathologists, mentioning that because the identity of the person was already confirmed, a thorough procedure was less necessary. Even further, the hot temperatures of the day and the pungent smell of the corpse was an additional motivation that fortunately led to cutting the autopsy short. In the end, Haselden got the doctors to issue a death certificate with their signatures that labeled the cause of death as drowning and that the body had been at sea for 8-10 days.

However, despite the final result being death by drowning for over a week, there were things that bothered the doctor. Dr. Fernández recalled on nearly all other drowned victims a form of nibbling on the earlobes and flesh by sea animals. Additionally, the clothes of a drowned man in the water for that duration would usually have become a nearly amorphous form, and the hair would usually be extremely brittle. However, he observed none of these characteristics, with no form of nibbling on the skin or ears, wet clothes but not formless, and still seemingly "shiny" hair. Unfortunately, it is uncertain how many of these doubts and peculiarities were mentioned because the report was burned in a fire in 1976, but it is terrifying to consider what would've happened if he had just a little more time to examine the body.

Major William Martin was buried the next day in Huelva with full military honors under the fake name. However, while the body was buried, the items found with the corpse were to be put in a different place. For the time being, the Spanish held onto the briefcase and other personal items. After intercepting all the communications between Haselden and Montagu, the German Abwehr agents were quite eager to look inside the briefcase.

Surprisingly, however, the Spanish actually refused to hand the briefcase over. The Spanish sent the briefcase instead to their headquarters at San Fernando in the province of Cadiz on May 5th. The briefcase was held there and waiting to be sent to Madrid. However, Germans with strong ties were able to pressure the Spanish authorities into opening the case and photographing some of the contents, although the envelopes, which contained the actual fake plans, were not opened. Ironically the Spanish were following the correct procedure the one time the Allies wished they didn't.

Luckily, with maximum pressure in Madrid, the Germans were able to force the Spanish to turn over the documents. This effort was led by Karl-Erich Kühlenthal, a high-ranking Abewehr who was assigned to Spain. He was in direct contact with Wilhelm Canaris, the head of the Abwehr intelligence. Karl-Erich had to ask Canaris personally to get involved and pressure the Spanish officials for this case.

The Axis Take the Bait

After much effort, the German Abwehr could finally scan the documents. However, despite their eagerness and anticipation, they still had to be extraordinarily careful with the contents and make it look as if it were never opened. After carefully removing the notes from the envelopes, which were still damp from the sea, they dried them and took photographs. After processing and reviewing all the materials, the Spanish put the letters into saltwater once more to hide any traces of tampering and drying. Despite the carefulness of the Spanish, they had no way of knowing that the British spies had planted an eyelash, which was now gone.

By May 8th, the German intelligence knew of the entire fake "operation." Karl Erich Kühlenthal took the information and brought the information to Germany himself. Then, the documents in the suitcase were compiled and returned, sent first to Haselden, then back to London.

One of the biggest questions of the whole operation was why exactly Karl-Erich Kühlenthal was so convinced of the body's legitimacy. He knew the inspection was shallow and should have been more cautious and reserved about the information.

The British had their own ideas and theories as to why it happened. The leading theory among the British is that Karl-Erich was of partial Jewish background. It turns out that his grandmother was Jewish, and any familial connection to the Jewish was an issue for German officers. Most likely, he was desperate to prove himself, and those documents were exactly what he needed to show it. Whatever the reason, his strong belief in the Operation is one of the key reasons it succeeded.

R.C. BREAD

CHAPTER 5: THE INVASION OF SICILY

Once the British had the case that belonged to William Martin, they immediately conducted a thorough investigation of it. Firstly and most importantly, they had noticed that the eyelash was gone. Not only that, but subtle details further hinted that there was tampering with the case. The letters had subtle signs of being refolded, found by the damage to the paper fibers. Then, when the letters were dried up they took a rolled shape, which indicated the Spaniards' method of removing them from envelopes. It was certain that at least someone had gone through the suitcase. The members of Operation Mincemeat then communicated back with Haselden through open and intercepted communication lines that said that there was no sign of the suitcase being opened or tampered with, to hide any suspicions from the Germans.

By May 14th, the Allies intercepted German communication that confirmed they had read the letters of the suitcase and even had discussions about what to do next. One particular comment that the Allies intercepted was concrete proof of the deception succeeding. General Jodl, the Chief of Operations Staff, said on a telephone to Rome, "You can forget about Sicily, we know it is in Greece." The Axis powers had completely fallen for the false plan and were convinced of an incoming Allied invasion of Greece through the Balkans.

Even though the Germans were convinced, Montagu and his team still had to maintain the lie and ensure that nobody would be suspicious of William Martin and his identity. They made sure to put his name in the list of British casualties in the Times newspaper in early June of 1943, in case anyone happened to look. In a stroke of luck, other casualties resulting from plane crashes were listed that day. The article showed that the Luftwaffe happened to attack and down British aircraft close to Spanish territorial waters within a time window that fit nearly perfectly well into the lie of Operation Mincemeat. The deal was sealed.

The Movement in Response to Operation Mincemeat

The information taken from Huelva made its way up the German chain of command. Each individual was more and more cautious of the lie, but the level of exactness and precision the deception was created with made it so it eventually made it all the way to the top. By May of 1943, the highest levels of Nazi leadership discussed the new information from Huelva. The meeting held prominent figures, such as Karl Donitz, the German Grand Admiral, and Adolf Hitler.

Donitz had returned from Italy, where he met Mussolini and informed him of the new information. However, Mussolini firmly thought that the Allies were creating a ruse and that they instead were going to invade Italy. Mussolini protested, but Hitler and Donitz were set on the Balkans and Greece and disregarded his claims.

The German Fuhrer began to make movements in order to defend the Balkans based on the information he received from Huelva. Hitler moved important troops and sections there, most notably the 1st Panzer Division, which was a seasoned and battle-hardened unit. They were stationed in Thessaloniki in Greek Macedonia instead of France. This movement of troops was intercepted by the Allies, and thus they knew that the Germans were making preparations for the supposed Greek invasion.

In addition to the 1st Panzer being relocated from France, Hitler also pulled two entire Panzer divisions from the Eastern Front, where the USSR and the Axis forces were fighting. In that way, the

Operation indirectly helped by relieving pressure and fighting on the Eastern Front. There were also numerous torpedo submarines and boats moved from Sicily to Greece, and this would end up saving the lives of many Allied troops that would eventually cross the Mediterranean Sea. By the end of all these employments, nearly seven divisions would be moved to Greece, six more than what was originally there.

In other sections of the Balkans, the Germans relocated an additional ten divisions. Before this migration, there were a lot of internal conflicts and mostly on the sidelines in the war, but soon it escalated into something much larger and became a hotspot of German military, defense planning, and activity, all due to Operation Mincemeat.

Operation Husky - The Invasion of Sicily

The invasion of Sicily, codenamed Operation Husky, was set to happen on July 9th of 1943. The German's slow response to this invasion was perhaps the best testament to how successful Operation Mincemeat was. Allied intelligence made sure to intercept as much German communication as the invasion progressed.

The lie was so convincing that Hitler continued to act on it even after the Allied forces started to attack. Four hours after the invasion started, a Luftwaffe was seen relocating to Sardinia. Hitler continued to make moves toward defending the Balkans until the last week of July, nearly three weeks after the invasion started. The famous German General, Erwin Rommel, nicknamed the Desert Fox, was reassigned to Thessaloniki and tasked with organizing the German defense against an attack that would never come. The agreement among historians is that Hitler and his high command didn't realize they were being duped until it was way too late to reorganize and change the course of the Allied invasion.

By July 25th of 1943, around 16 days after the start of the

invasion, Mussolini found himself in a political disaster. The gains made by the Allies created lots of pressure, which turned out badly for Benito Mussolini. The Grand Council of Fascism passed measures to limit his powers, and he lost control of the Italian military. Now the militarized control returned to Italian King Victor Emmanuel III, who was sidelined by Mussolini up until this time. On July 26th, the King removed Mussolini from power as prime minister and was arrested, making Germany lose a major ally.

During the invasion, the resistance was led by the Germans, and only had a force of around 60,000 troops to do it. At the Allies' peak, they had more than 460,000 men invading. Despite the vast numerical difference, the German forces had considerable success in slowing down the Allies advance. Even though the battle ended in complete Axis defeat, it was also a minor strategic victory for the Germans since they bought enough time to evacuate their personnel to the Italian peninsula. Overall though, the battle resulted in a collapse of a major ally of Germany, Mussolini, and a full Allied occupation of Sicily.

Even though Mussolini later escaped the prison through support from the German Special Forces, Operation Husky undoubtedly left a devastating blow to the Axis powers in the Mediterranean. The Allies were now able to regroup and use Sicily as a gathering area for the final push into Italy to create another front to enter closer to Nazi Germany. The island was secured some five weeks after the invasion began, on August 17th of 1943.

Although Operation Mincemeat and Operation Barclay (a series of fake military maneuvers to trick the Axis powers into thinking the next attack was in Greece) definitely helped with Operation Husky, other factors contributed to the success of Operation Husky. That was the poor coordination between the Germans and Italians. The fact that Hitler completely dismissed Mussolini's concerns about an Allied ruse further showed the lack of communication between these two groups. Had there been a more respectful and a more understanding relationship between the two, it would have been possible the Operation would have failed.

R.C. BREAD

CHAPTER 6: POST-WAR LIFE

As Mussolini's reign crumbled under the attack on Sicily, a new government was formed. From thereon, the Italian government began to gradually and secretly negotiate with the Allies to eventually exit the war. According to some historians, like Michael Howard, a British military historian, Operation Mincemeat was probably the most successful deceptive operation of World War II. Nevertheless, he also believed that Operation Mincemeat, nor any other deceptive mission had as many consequences as Hitler's own delusions. Howard wasn't the only one who thought that Hitler's focus on the Balkans was nearly an obsession.

One major way the military thought of success was through casualties of a battle or war. Operation Husky was most definitely successful in this regard. It had a low number of casualties, losses, and a shorter duration. It was thought that 10,000 men would be taken out of action within the first week, but only about a 7th of that was lost in total. The naval command expected 300 ships to be lost, but only 12 were lost in the end. Lastly, they thought it would take 90 days for the invasion to finish, but instead, it only took 38. It was quite a strong testament to the impact of Operation Mincemeat.

Even further, Operation Husky had other large repercussions on the war. Due to the large invasion, Hitler put the invasion of Kursk on hold until July 13th, allowing the Russian forces a bit of breathing room and allowed them to prepare. In return, the USSR won the Battle of Kursk, completely shifting the tide as it was Hitler's last true attempt to regain the initiative on the Eastern Front after his failure at Stalingrad. The new front that was opened near Italy further forced the Axis powers to dedicate more forces and spread them out, which opened the gate for the eventual Operation Overlord, which would be the Allies' turning point in the war. Lastly, it took out the major Axis power: Italy, and reduced Hitler's power. It was a successful invasion, and was only truly made possible through the efforts of the agents of Operation Mincemeat

People After the War

There were many individuals who were crucial to the success of Operation Mincemeat. After the war, although they were all linked to the single mission, they led very different lives.

Ewen Montagu

Born on March 19th, 1901, Ewen Montagu was the second son of the wealthy Jewish Louis Montagu. He had two brothers: Stuart Montagu and Ivor Montagu. Stuart, as the eldest, perfectly fit the mold for the heir of the family. Meanwhile, Ivor followed a completely different path. Ivor later became a communist (and was later confirmed to have been a Russian spy during the Second World War) but had other significant impacts, such as popularizing table tennis through the creation of numerous national and international ping-pong organizations.

For his formal education, Ewen Montagu went to Westminster, Cambridge, and Harvard. It was during these years that he found his wife, Iris Solomon. Ewen and Iris had two children together: one son and one daughter. After his education, he became a lawyer, where he learned to enjoy the mental battles against his opponent in court. These sorts of mental battles came to help him later as he eventually went into counterintelligence.

During the war, he was separated from his family. Because his family was Jewish, he advised his wife and children to move to

America, where they would be out of the Nazis' reach. After the war, however, they were reunited again.

Post World War II, he returned to his occupation as a judge and also became a Judge Advocate of the Fleet, who supervised the courts related to the Royal Navy. Due to the success of Operation Mincemeat and his work in counterespionage, Montagu was designated as an Officer of the Order of the British Empire. He further continued his Jewish faith by becoming acting President of the United Synagogue and the President of the Anglo-Jewish Association.

In 1953, he wrote a documentary of Operation Mincemeat, titled *The Man Who Never Was*, which later became a film in 1956. It quickly became a global book and forever solidified Operation Mincemeat as one of the most interesting missions to have occurred.

After living a long and fulfilling life, Ewen Montagu died at 84 years old on July 19th of 1985.

Charles Cholmondeley

Charles Cholmondeley was born on January 27th, 1917. It was found that he always wanted to fly as a pilot in the Royal Air Force, but could never actually do it due to his massive height of 6'3" in combination with his poor eyesight. This would lead him to instead be referred to the MI5, where he eventually worked on Operation Mincemeat.

Charles's life is one of the most secret of the agents in Operation Mincemeat, which most likely stems from his desire to not be well known. One of the few accounts of Charles's life after the war is by Ben Macintyre. In his book about Operation Mincemeat, it mentions that he joined a unit in the Middle East that tried to destroy the locust population. Meanwhile, it is also suspected he worked with the MI5 and used the anti-locust unit as a cover. Then, after he finished his duties in the MI5, he moved, married, and started a business where he sold "horticultural machinery."

Similarly to Montagu, he was awarded an award and became a Member of the Order of the British Empire.

Charles died on June 15th of 1982, at 65 years of age. According to Macintyre, his tombstone only bears the initials "C.C.C.", further showing the secrecy around Charles.

Jean Leslie (AKA "Pam")

Jean Leslie was born on November 20th, 1923. While she had no structured education, it is thought that her proficiency in French helped with her occupation in the MI5 in 1941. Her role was to look through reports from Camp 020, where Axis agents were interrogated, and to relay any interesting or important information to her superiors.

After the war, she went on to marry Colonel William Gerard Leigh (and became Jean Leigh) in November of 1946, three years after Operation Mincemeat. The couple was often found traveling frequently and sharing a love for cocktails and creating such cocktails.William Leigh was a member of the Life Guards and the chairman of the Guards Polo Club, and later became famous for stopping a polo ball from hitting the Queen in 1971. Meanwhile, Jean Leigh became a talented gardener and frequently helped with charity work. Together, the two had a total of four children: two sons and two daughters.

When Ewen Montagu published his book about Operation Mincemeat, he made sure to first ask Jean Leigh in 1951 for permission to use her photo. However, It wasn't until 1996 that Jean Leigh publicly confirmed that she was the fake fiancée of William Martin.

Her husband, Colonel William Leigh, died in 2008. Jean Leigh died four years after, at the age of 88 years, on April 3rd, 2012.

Ian Fleming

Fleming was born on May 28th, 1908. He was born to a wealthy family and had his formal education at Eton and Sandhurst. His first career was mainly as a journalist, but the Second World War soon drastically shifted his life, where he was eventually put in the MI5.

While in the MI5, Vice-Admiral Godfrey released a paper known as "the Trout Memo," which contained the idea behind Operation Mincemeat. While released by Godfrey, Ian Fleming is credited with the ideas due to the document being written much more in his style.

While Fleming played a massive role in the duties of World War II, he is much more well known for what he did after the war: writing and starting the James Bond series. He wrote the globally known stories of James Bond, a secret agent. The novels he wrote were highly controversial at the time, which might have been the reason why his books rose to such fame.

Fleming wrote the novels until 1964, when he died of a heart attack at age 56. Even after his death, people still write stories to continue his series, and movies are still being produced that are from the James Bond series.

Glyndwr Michael

The identity of the body that fooled the Germans in the lead-up to the invasion of Sicily remained unknown for decades. Ewen Montagu refused to reveal the true name behind the body, despite many who asked. Montagu simply said that the vagrant was more or less a nobody and that "the only worthwhile thing he ever did was after his death."

The body remained unidentified until 1996, 11 years after Montagu's death, when it was revealed by amateur historian Roger

Morgan. Morgan was sifting through the Public Record Office in London and found information that identified Glyndwr Michael as the man behind the corpse.

However, despite the body being in the records, there are still some alternative theories in regards to the identity of the corpse. These theories originate from the book *The Secrets of the HMS Dasher* and a documentary produced by Colin Gibbons. They detail how the physical state of the homeless vagrant (Glyndwr Michael) would have been easily identified by pathologist Dr. Fernández. Furthermore, they explain how strange it is that Montagu and Cholmondeley had to drive all the way to Scotland to meet Jewell's crew. That would have caused unnecessary decomposition of the body, and it is thought that they went to Scotland for a different reason.

The port they went to was where the sunken victims of the HMS Dasher were being recovered. The HMS Dasher led to nearly 400 deaths and numerous bodies that went missing. The documentary and book regarding this theory explain that it is quite possible that Montagu and Cholmondeley realized how hard it would be to pass Glyndwr as a soldier killed in battle and instead used a real soldier, one from the sunken HMS Dasher. This also fits perfectly into the timeline and would lead to a quick change for them. While most historians disregard this theory (due to the documentation of Glyndwr Michael's name in the historical records), the feeling of mild mystery surrounding the body's identity adds an additional layer of intrigue to the story.

The body still lies in a grave under the number 1886 at the San Marco part of the Nuestra Senora cemetery in Huelva. The tombstone still has Major William Martin's name on it, but is more like a resting place for two people: one fake and one real. For a man that never existed, Major Martin certainly left his impact on history, but it's also important to look at the true man, the real one (the one acknowledged by most historians), who unknowingly donated his body to this cause.

The real story of Glyndwr Michael is not one of fame and honor but one of misery and suffering. He was a poor Welsh vagrant that died from consuming rat poison in an abandoned warehouse. Had Operation Mincemeat not happened, he would have simply been another death, another tomb in the cemetery, another record in history. He would have been an unknown man who died soundlessly like so many others. Yet, he was brought to fame.

Montagu's secrecy of Glyndwr Michael's identity was not simply preference but was because he promised to never reveal the identity for as long as he lived. He never even revealed the fact that he was a man with no family and instead said that the body had only been used after securing permission from his parents, which has been largely disproven.

Since Martin's reveal as Glyndwr Michael, the world has learned a lot more about his life. He was found to be born in Aberbargoed, a small town in the Welsh County of Monmouth. His backstory and history was also a depressing story. His father was a coal miner and committed suicide when Glyndwr was only 15. He continued to live with his mother and worked at an early age finding any manual labor and jobs he could find. He lived this way until his mother passed away when he was 31.

His life continued to get darker and darker. Afterward, he decided to move to London and lived on the streets. Eventually, he decided to end his life and ingested a large amount of phosphorous rat poison. He was found alive and brought to the St. Pancras Hospital, but there was nearly nothing that the doctors could do at that point. He died two days after consuming the rat poison and died at the age of 34. Historians generally believe that it was a case of suicide, but another theory that arose was that Glyndwr Michael simply ate the poison by accident. People often put such rat poison on bread, and so it's possible that the hungry and homeless Glyndwr Michael found such bread and quickly ate it.

Glyndwr Michael lived a life of suffering and pain. However, while he died a homeless vagrant, he is forever in history books. He is an unlikely story of an unknown, belated hero. He found a way to impact the world not in his life, but in his death.

Thank you for your service, Glyndwr Michael.

The Tomb of Glyndwr Michael; image from wikemedia commons by Benutzer:smasheng

https://commons.wikimedia.org/wiki/File:William_Martin.jpg

R.C. BREAD

Hi! How Did You Enjoy My Novella About Operation Mincemeat?

If you have time, can you please let me know your thoughts on it by writing a review? Any review is welcome, as it will help me to improve this book and ones in the future.

Also, if you enjoyed this book, or want to be informed about future books that I publish, please email rcbreadhistory@gmail.com. By emailing this email, and simply typing "join," you will be updated to have exclusive access to information regarding any new books that I am working on and researching.
(my next book is going to be about the heroic act of a certain group of student soldeirs)

Once again, thank you so much for your time and support!

REFERENCES

'Perhaps the most successful single deception operation of the entire war. (2019). History TV. https://www.history.co.uk/article/operation-mincemeat

Glyndwr Michael. (n.d.). Military Wiki. https://military.wikia.org/wiki/Glyndwr_Michael

Glyndwr Michael. (n.d.). Today in History He. Retrieved July 6, 2021, from https://todayinhistory.blog/tag/glyndwr-michael/

MICHAEL, GLYNDWR ("Major William Martin, RN") (1909-1943), "the man who never was" | Dictionary of Welsh Biography. (n.d.). Biography. Wales. Retrieved July 6, 2021, from https://biography.wales/article/s8-MICH-GLY-1909

Operation Mincemeat: How a dead tramp fooled Hitler. (2010, December 3). BBC News. https://www.bbc.com/news/magazine-11887115

The amazing Operation Mincemeat: Ian Fleming devised a WWII plan to fool the Nazis. (2018, July 4). The Vintage News. https://www.thevintagenews.com/2018/07/04/operation-mincemeat/

The Man Who Never Was - The True Story of Glyndwr Michael. (n.d.). Www.themanwhoneverwas.com. Retrieved July 6, 2021, from http://www.themanwhoneverwas.com/

Operation Mincemeat: How a Dead Man and a Bizarre Plan Fooled the Nazis and Assured an Allied Victory, (2010, January 18). Erenow. https://erenow.net/ww/operation-mincemeat/

Fly Fishing (2012, April 4). Blogger. http://thepublici.blogspot.com/2012/04/fly-fishing.html

Operation Mincemeat: The Story Behind "The Man Who Never Was" in Operation Husky (2013, September 9). Defense Media Network. https://www.defensemedianetwork.com/stories/operation-mincemeat-the-story-behind-the-man-who-never-war-in-operation-husky/

The amazing Operation Mincemeat: Ian Fleming devised a WWII Plan to fool the Nazis (2018, July 4). Vintage News. https://www.thevintagenews.com/2018/07/04/operation-mincemeat/

World War II... Operation Mincemeat (2021, July 8). Blogger. http://

whitealmond-privatesicily.blogspot.com/2021/07/operation-mincemeat.html

Tricks of the War Trade (2004, August 24). The Washington Post. https://www.washingtonpost.com/archive/lifestyle/2004/08/24/tricks-of-the-war-trade/e4929511-b4bb-41e2-975a-129324082476/

Behind new film 'Operation Mincemeat,' true story of WWII's greatest deception (2022, April 15). The Times of Israel. https://www.timesofisrael.com/behind-new-film-operation-mincemeat-the-true-story-of-wwiis-greatest-deception/

The Mincemeat Postmortem: Forensic Aspects of World War II's Boldest Counterintelligence Operation (2009, February). Research Gate. https://www.researchgate.net/publication/24009553_The_Mincemeat_Postmortem_Forensic_Aspects_of_World_War_II%27s_Boldest_Counterintelligence_Operation

How a blind racer turned secret agent and helped defeat the Nazis (2013, November 12). Road Track. https://www.roadandtrack.com/car-culture/a5955/john-jock-horsfall-works-driver-secret-agent/

The photo that FOOLED Hitler: How MI5 secretary's beach snap was planted with fake plans about Allied invasion Greece on corpse that was dumped in the Med under Operation Mincemeat (2022, April 13). Daily Mail. https://www.dailymail.co.uk/news/article-10714251/How-MI5-secretarys-beach-snap-planted-Operation-Mincemeat-dupe-Hitler.html

Hook, line and sinker: How did Operation Mincemeat work? (2022, April 16). Caution Spoilers. https://www.cautionspoilers.com/re-caps-spoiler-warning/hook-line-and-sinker-did-operation-mincemeat-work/

What was Operation Mincemeat? (n.d.). Imperial War Museum. https://www.iwm.org.uk/history/the-war-on-paper-operation-mincemeat

Printed in Great Britain
by Amazon

34463105R00036